AN ADVENT PRAYER JOURNAL

PRAYING BENEATH THE TREE

FAITHFULLYFOLLOWINGMINISTRIES.ORG

Dedication

This book is dedicated to the memory of my son,
Ryan Thomas.
I am ever grateful for the 22 years we shared
together before Jesus welcomed you home.
Your fingerprints are all over my heart.
Thank you for always cheering your momma
forward and reminding me to smile.

Endorsements

Beautifully written with stories that will touch your heart, this guide is a wonderful (but realistic) reminder of practical ways to keep the focus on Christ this Christmas. With humor, candor, and always grace, Jodie Barrett encourages like no other. Her come alongside you attitude makes it feel as if a close friend is helping you to get the balance back in your life this Christmas season. I'm looking forward to following her guide this year as I take a step back from all that sparkles and remember to focus on the practical ways Jodie encourages us to plug into others.

Laura Adams, Designer, writer, and speaker at
lauraadamscreative.net

Jodie Barrett truly lives her faith, and prayer is an integral part of everything she does. I know I struggle with the Christmas season sometimes—as much as I love God, I have trouble keeping my focus on the meaning behind Christmas, and I can get caught up in all the décor and busyness and forget that we are doing all of this because God is truly with us. What a gift. With Jingle and Joy, Jodie has hit upon a meaningful way to bring out the beauty and joy of the season and deepen our relationship with God at the same time. This book will become a regular part of my Christmas traditions.

Kelly O'Dell Stanley, author of
Praying Upside Down: A Creative Prayer Experience to Transform Your Time with God and *Designed to Pray: Creative Ways to Engage with God.*

In the years that I've had the privilege of knowing Jodie Barrett there is one word that consistently presents itself when her name pops up...joy. I'm grateful that the joy which emanates from Jodie's ministry, her words and life is the kind of joy that you and I can identify with because it's honest. Jodie is authentic when it comes to how challenging life can be and yet she never wavers in the message that there is always joy to be found. *Jingle and Joy* is the perfect blend of the honest admission that Christmas can be overwhelming, but that joy is the greatest gift the season has to offer. This book will be on my nightstand this Christmas season!

Cindy K. Krall - *Speaker, blogger, freelance writer at cindykrall.com*

JOY oozes from Jodie Barrett's soul as she conveys her message of advent in *Jingle and Joy*. She reminds us that getting caught up in the busyness of life can cause us to miss out on the most beautiful season of the year. Jesus is the greatest gift of all and this book provides a meaningful and relevant perspective to keep us grounded all year long. *Jingle and Joy* will be a favorite for years to come.

Mitzi Neely—Author of *A Thankful Heart: 30 Days to the Grateful Life* and *Dwell in the Psalms*.

Jingle and Joy— Praying Beneath the Tree

A 25 Day Advent Prayer Journal

Copyright © 2018 by Faithfully Following Ministries
All rights reserved.

www.FaithfullyFollowing.com

ISBN: 978-1729471333
Independently Published by: Kindle Direct Publishing

Devotions written by: Jodie Barrett
Cover Design by: Jana Kennedy-Spicer
Interior Design by: Jana Kennedy-Spicer
www.SweetToTheSoul.com

Contents

Introduction

Standing three feet tall, filled with anticipation, right beside my daddy, I was one happy little girl. We were off to find a Christmas tree at the corner lot. Daddy and I go way back! For as long as I can remember I've been a Daddy's girl and I've loved Christmas trees just as long. This was going to be a great day!

My mind fails on all the details of that day at the tree lot, but I imagine we cased the place in search of the perfect tree. One just the right size, with a strong, straight trunk, and lively needles. The salesman pulling out each tree I pointed to, placing it upright, letting Daddy and me peer at its beauty until we were satisfied and said, "Yes, that's the one!"

I assume others and their families were doing the same. Those details are fuzzy, but I clearly remember being right beside my Daddy seeking the perfect tree to take home for Christmas. Imagine my surprise when I looked up, clinging to my Daddy's britches leg, only to see it wasn't my daddy's face attached to the leg I was holding onto tightly. Somewhere in the process I was fooled by someone that looked very much like my daddy.

I grasped onto him, because that was where I wanted to be... right beside my Father, preparing for Christmas. Only, in the jingle of things, I was lost.

Isn't that how Christmas can be sometimes?

We set out with our hearts focused on our Father preparing for the Christmas season. Our intention is to celebrate and

INTRODUCTION

honor His Son, our Savior.
*"The Savior--yes, the Messiah, the Lord- has been
born today in Bethlehem, the city of David!"*
Luke 2:11 NLT

We are grateful for a gift freely given. The birth of Jesus warrants a time of reflection and celebration. But somewhere, somehow "the jingle" takes our joy, our focus gets shifted from Jesus to the world, and we become lost. Suddenly, we look up, expecting to see the smile of our Daddy, only to find we are not even close to Him.

We get wrapped up in ribbon, tangled up in lights, distracted by traditions that were meant to help us keep Christ the center of Christmas, only to find the world has won our affection and attention. Furthermore, many of us will lose the joy of the season as we let the hoopla drain us physically, financially, and yes, spiritually.

Join me on a journey. One that led me to the foot of a Christmas tree and carried me back to focusing on a manger and the babe that was born for you and me. Each day we will walk through scripture and pray. We will keep some traditions, like putting up Christmas trees, but maybe, just maybe, a little slower, a little more intentional, and a little less distracted.

WE CAN HAVE

a little jingle and a whole lotta joy

AS WE KEEP CHRIST
THE CENTER OF CHRISTMAS·

Jingle and Joy ~ Praying Beneath the Tree

Scripture Reading List

1. Pray for all people - 1 Timothy 2:1
2. Pray for your neighbors - Luke 10:27
3. Pray for the homeless - Isaiah 25:4
4. Pray for those who work day and night - Luke 2:8
5. Pray for the difficult people - Luke 1:47-49
6. Pray for marriages - Matthew 1:19-20
7. Pray with and for your children - Proverbs 22:6
8. Pray for the grieving - 2 Corinthians 1:3-4
9. Pray for a student - Luke 2:52
10. Pray for the lost - John 3:16-17
11. Pray for the sick - Luke 1:37
12. Pray for teachers- 1 Thessalonians 5:11
13. Pray for missionaries - Isaiah 52:7
14. Pray for caregivers- Matthew 11:28
15. Pray for peace (inner) - John 14:27
16. Pray for the military- Psalm 18:29
17. Pray for the lonely - Psalm 68:6
18. Pray for leaders - 1 Timothy 2:1-3
19. Pray for retail workers - James 1:19
20. Pray for those battling addiction - Psalm 31:1-2
21. Pray for those with depression - Psalm 143:7-8
22. Pray for a coworker- Colossians 3:23
23. Pray for the fragile - Luke 2:7
24. Pray for forgiveness- John 3:16-17
25. Praise God for Jesus - Luke 2:11-15
26. Continue lifting prayers - Psalm 5:3

Week One

Prayer Tree 1-2-3

1-2-3 start your prayer tree:

The last thing you need is a complicated process in an already busy season. I will keep this super simple! Because really, it's less about the tree and more about the prayer.

First, a little background. Several years ago, a friend shared how she would slowly unpack her ornaments and hang them prayerfully on the tree as she remembered others in prayer. That year as I decorated my tree I did the same. I was amazed at how the process prepared my heart for Christmas and inspired me to be intentional about praying for others! After that I began looking for ornaments that reminded me to pray for certain people and things. Then while my husband was deployed at Christmas I began sitting under the tree longer and invited others to join me. One year later I wanted a specific focus to help me keep the purpose of the prayer tree first and foremost. God led me to 1 Timothy 2:1 which reads, *"I urge you, first of all, to pray for all people."* The urgency of this verse and directive to pray for all people guided me to stay focused on the purpose, rather than the process.

Here's the 1-2-3

1. Grab a notebook, your bible, and maybe even some tags to write on and hang on the tree. Your notebook will help you track your many prayers. Your bible will help you pray scripture for others. Use the tags to write names/needs on and hang them on the tree. When you pass by and see a name or a need you will remember to pray.

2. Pick a time of day when you pause beneath the tree and pray for others. I picked evening because the lights are glowing, and the day is slowing, but any time is perfect.

3. Pray each day being intentional to include others. Those you know and those you do not know. Use the prayer prompts in this book to help you pray for others each day.

Optional:
Keep a basket of ornaments below the tree and hang one each day as you pray for others. You will be surprised how many ornaments you have that already hold meaning. If you wish, you can add to your collection purchasing ornaments that remind you to think of others.

No room for another tree? Use the tree you have and add the prayer tags. No room for any tree, keep a prayer journal.

Lord, Thank you for this time of year. It's a time we often give gifts to one another in celebration of your son's birthday. Let this be the year we give the gift of prayer. The year we slow the pace, clear the distractions, and embrace the joy. In Jesus' name, Amen.

PRAYER TREE 1-2-3

Lord
THANK YOU
FOR ALLOWING
Your children
TO
COME &
LAY THEIR REQUESTS AT
YOUR
feet
amen

PRAY EXPECTANTLY FOR ALL PEOPLE

"I urge you, first of all, to pray for all people." 1 Timothy 2:1 NLT

We pray with honest and open hearts. We pray bringing our hearts to Jesus. We pray to comfort others. We pray to a BIG God who does BIG things. We pray expectantly.

Does it seem too bold to expect God to respond?

He asks us to come and bring our burdens. He asks us to come and share our concerns. He asks us to come and confess our sins. He asks us to pray for others.

> *And, we can expect.*
> ⇒ Expect God to hear us.
> ⇒ Expect God to respond.
> ⇒ Expect God to answer.
> ⇒ TRUST God to be God.

Psalm 61:1-2 NLT says, *"O God, listen to my cry! Hear my prayer! From the ends of the earth, I cry to you for help."* There is an urgency in the psalmist's voice. A call for help. A cry lifted to the one we know and trust can help.

It's how He desires us to come. He wants us to turn to the One who can do more than we ask or imagine (Ephesians 3:20)! And as we come to Him with expectant hearts we also come with hearts filled with praise. Psalm 61:8 NLT says, *"Sing praises to your name forever as I fulfill my vows each day."*

As we kneel beneath our prayer trees each day, kneel expectantly. Kneel with prayerful hearts. Kneel with hearts filled with praise and pray expectantly for all people.

EXPECTANTLY

Lord, Thank you for being a God who listens. A God with open doors awaiting our knock. A God who loves, forgives, comforts, and strengthens His people. Thank you for allowing your children to come and lay their requests at your feet. We thank you now for all you will do in response to our prayers. Amen.

day 1

Lord
HELP US
love
OUR
NEIGHBORS
well

amen

PRAY FOR YOUR NEIGHBORS

We were excited to build a new home and move into a new neighborhood but not everyone welcomed us with open arms. One new neighbor was less than welcoming. It hurt.

I remember being disappointed and even angry. I remember a good friend being upset for our family. And then, it happened. My neighbor greeted me with a hug and said, "I'm so sorry, will you forgive me?"

Now every time that neighbor sees me she either prays with me, asks how she can pray for our family, or tells me how she's praying for us.

Neighbors. Some we love and some we, well, have a hard time loving. But God is clear. It's so important for us to love Him and our neighbors. Those next door, those down the road, those next to us in line, and those beside us in church.

"Love the Lord with all your heart, all your soul, all your strength, and all your mind.' And, 'Love your neighbor as yourself.'"
Luke 10:27 NIV

Today, pray for your neighbors. Those you know and those you do not. Those who are kind and those who have hurt you.

How can we pray for our neighbors?
- Ask God to bless them and keep them.
- Ask God to strengthen them and protect them.
- Ask God to reveal how you can be a good neighbor.
- Ask God to heal any hurt there is between you and your neighbors.

NEIGHBORS

Lord, Your words are important to us. We want to live them to the fullest. Today we lift our neighbors to you. Bless them. Help us be a blessing to them. Restore broken relationships. Help us ask for forgiveness where it is needed. Bridge gaps! Mend fences! Help us love our neighbors well. Amen.

day 2

Lord
SHOW US
WHEN & HOW
TO help
OTHERS

amen

Jingle and Joy ~ Praying Beneath the Tree

PRAY FOR THE HOMELESS

We live in a small town. Most people know about "the man under the bridge." We all have different names for him but we all seem to know who he is.

Many have tried to offer aid. Sometimes it's well received, and other times not. I happen to drive past his "home" every day on the way to work. I struggled with knowing how to help until I sensed the Spirit's prompting.

Pray.

"I urge you, FIRST OF ALL, to pray for all people."
1 Timothy: 2:1 NLT

First, pray. Pray for all people.

Have you ever said, "all we can do now is pray"? I know I have. We don't necessarily mean it's last on the list, but we do sometime discount the power of prayer. Prayer changes things.

Prayer impacts the lives of others.

That day God prompted me to pray for the man beneath the bridge. Rather than the complicated list of things I was processing about how to help, He simply wanted me to pray first. This season when we see others without shelter ask God to be their shelter.

"But you are a tower of refuge to the poor, O Lord,
a tower of refuge to the needy in distress.
You are a refuge from the storm
and a shelter from the heat."
Isaiah 24:4 NLT
25

How can we pray for the homeless?

- Ask God to be their shelter and refuge.
- Ask God to lead them to a safe place.
- Ask God to provide food and clothing.
- Ask God how you can help, then respond in obedience.

Lord, We thank you and praise you for your love. Help us love others well. Let that love begin with prayer. Today we pray for those who live on the streets, in cars, on benches, and in-between places. Keep them safe. Shelter them beneath your wings. Protect them from the elements. We open our hearts to you, willing to be your hands and feet. Show us when and how to help. Amen.

day 3

Lord PROVIDE REST & POUR *blessings* OVER THOSE *work* WHO DAY & NIGHT.

amen

Jingle and Joy ~ Praying Beneath the Tree

PRAY FOR THOSE WHO WORK
DAY & NIGHT

Pray for those who work day and night.

◆ Law enforcement officers
◆ Health care workers
◆ Emergency services - Fire, Rescue
◆ Shift workers in plants and mills
◆ Truck drivers
◆ Mothers (they never take off, right?) and shepherds

Did that last one catch you off guard?

> *"And there were shepherds out in the fields nearby,*
> *keeping watch over their flocks at night."*
> Luke 2:8 NIV

Since the beginning of time there are those who work tirelessly, day and night. It requires going against the body's natural desire for rest. Many do it because they must, and others, because they want to. This type of work pulls us away from our families, takes a toll on our health, but it needs to be done. Hospitals cannot close at 5pm and reopen the next day, just like mommies can't say, "I'll take care of you in the morning."

How can we pray for those working day and night?

• Ask God to give them strength and good health.
• Ask God to keep them alert.
• Ask God to give them rest.
• Ask God to protect their family.
• Ask God how you can encourage them.

WORKERS

And those shepherds? Remember to thank God for being our Shepherd. He watches over His flock day and night. Rejoice!

Lord, You are our Shepherd. Thank you seems small. You watch over us; you are present day and night providing the way. We praise you. We come to lift others who work day and night. Some even lay their life down for others. Strengthen them! Protect them! Provide rest and pour blessings onto their families. Help us remember to encourage and support those who work around the clock to provide for our protection and comfort. We rejoice in knowing that You never take a day away from watching over Your flock. Amen .

· · · · · *day* 4

Lord

BRING

healing & HOPE

TO THE

Broken

AND

HURTING

amen

day 5

PRAY FOR THE DIFFICULT

The difficult situations.
The difficult relationships.
The difficult things to understand.
The difficult decisions we need to make.
The difficult times we hold tight.
The difficult people we need to love.
The difficult things we need to forgive.

Can you imagine how difficult it must have been for Mary, the mother of Jesus?

To hear she was pregnant. No husband yet. Knowing that she could be stoned because of how it looked to be pregnant and unwed.

Difficult decisions had to be made. Difficult questions had to be answered. She and Joseph had to remain faithful to God and one another even in the difficult.

Telling her parents must have been hard. Understanding would require deep faith. Waiting would require patience. Trusting God during the difficult would be vital.

During the difficult, Mary praised God.

"and my spirit rejoices in God my Savior,
for he has been mindful
of the humble state of his servant.
From now on all generations will call me blessed,
for the Mighty One has done great things for me—
holy is his name." Luke 1:47-49 NIV

THE DIFFICULT

Today pray for your own difficulties and the difficulties others face.

Mary was encouraged by her relative Elizabeth. We can be an encourager to someone walking through unknown, frightening times where faith is needed.

Lord, Your mercy never fails. Your strength is ever present. You fill the hungry! You help the hurting! You restore! We lift to you the difficult. Turn our hearts upward as we wait for resolutions. Keep our minds stayed on you and the goodness of your promises. Bring healing and hope into broken and hurting. Thank you, Lord. Amen .

day 5

Lord HELP US open OUR HEARTS TO YOU & invite YOU INTO OUR marriages

amen

WHISPER PRAYERS FOR MARRIAGES

There are a few ornaments of special churches I hang on my tree each year. One of the church my great grandmother took me to attend, and the other, the church my husband grew up in, and later where we said our marriage vows. One year while hanging them on the tree I thought, "How many marriages have taken place in these two places?"

I smiled thinking of my own. But here is something real...marriage is a blessing, but it can also be hard. Bringing together two imperfect people to live a lifetime together requires commitment, patience, love, and prayer.

Joseph was committed to Mary. It's hard not to see his love for her. Even before their marriage, when He learned Mary was pregnant, Joseph was loving and kind.

> *" Joseph, to whom she was engaged, was a righteous man*
> *and did not want to disgrace her publicly, so he decided to*
> *break the engagement quietly."*
> Matthew 1:19 NLT

The scriptures tell us he didn't disgrace her or leave her. But it did take God's intervention.

> *"As he considered this, an angel of the Lord appeared*
> *to him in a dream. "Joseph, son of David," the angel said,*
> *"do not be afraid to take Mary as your wife. For the child within*
> *her was conceived by the Holy Spirit."*
> Matthew 1:20 NLT

OUR MARRIAGES ARE STRONGER WITH GOD'S INTERVENTION AND GUIDANCE.

Even the most challenging times can lead to great blessings when we allow God to take control.

Are you married? Do you know someone who is or will be? Pray. Whisper prayers for marriage.

Lord, We rejoice in you today! You are worthy of praise! Much praise! Today we come and lift marriages. We admit, they can be beautiful and difficult at the same time. Help us open our hearts to you and invite you into our marriages. Appear to us and guide us through each day. Help us be loving, patient, kind, and forgiving. Give us times of great joy and laughter. For any marriage that is struggling, Lord, intervene. We know you are a God of relationship and you can restore even the most broken. Do a work of restoration for those who come, for those we lift. Amen

Jingle and Joy ~ Praying Beneath the Tree

day 6

Lord

HELP US

REMEMBER *You love* THAT

OUR CHILDREN

EVEN MORE

THAN

we DO.

amen

PRAY FOR AND WITH YOUR CHILDREN

May I be honest? Sometimes I look back and I want a "do over." My children are older, and I want to go back and pray with and for them more often. I cannot. But I can continue to pray now.

May I be honest again? There are times I wonder if it makes a difference. You know, those times you weep on your knees and it seems futile? That time is never wasted. Some situations take patience and others take trust.

CHILDREN NEED PRAYER. CHILDREN CAN PRAY. IN FACT, A CHILD'S PRAYER IS ONE OF THE *most honest things you will ever hear.*

I recently read about a father's recollection of his son's bedtime prayer. Earlier that day the father had come home with a new haircut and the son was less than impressed. That night, as they prayed together, the father said, "Let's pray for our family, for our home..." and his son interrupted, "and for your hair!"

Children don't hold anything back and they shouldn't. God asks for open and honest prayers.

I've had to explain to my young son why prayers don't always seem to get answered, but, if his grandmother ends her mealtime prayer without asking for protection over him and his sister, he proclaims, "MeMa, you aren't finished yet." He values prayer, even on the days I think he doesn't.

I'm thankful for others who pray for my children. As you pray for your own today, pray also for someone else's children.

> **"Direct your children onto the right path, and when they are older, they will not leave it."**
> Proverbs 22:6 NLT

Oh Lord, oh Lord, One of the most precious gifts you give, you place in our arms, and call them children. Fragile and strong, at the same time. May we be faithful to pray for and with our children. Many face battles we are completely unaware of. Be their mighty warrior. Fight on their behalf. Mold them and shape them. Dwell in their hearts. Consume them with your love. Be their peace, their hope, and their joy. When they rise, let us sing joyfully about who you are. When they sleep let us place our requests for them at the cross. Help us remember you love them even more than we do. You are their good, good, Father. Amen

day 7

Jingle and Joy ~ Praying Beneath the Tree

Week Two

Making Room for the Babe

Hurry here, hurry there! Everywhere I turn there seems to be hurry.

Something strange happens after September. We begin this strange countdown as we watch the retail stores fill with lights and decorations. My heart pounds as I see posts on Facebook proclaiming how many days are left before Christmas. Thanksgiving is often overlooked or even forgotten.

The roadways become congested, the grocery store aisles have pile ups, and all I can say is it seems we become exhausted while we race to complete endless to-do lists that are all about Christmas. Well, at least the Christmas we have grown accustomed to celebrating. One filled with commercialism, Pinterest boards, and expensive gift giving.

Slow down, pause, rewind and remember.

Several years ago, I began preparing my heart for the celebration of Christmas by doing an Advent study. I was amazed at the results. Why had I failed to do this before? Lingering in God's word each day ushered peace into my heart and taught me to wait for Christmas with anticipation. I learned to prepare my heart to see His goodness and, in the wait, to watch for His hand at work. I had to make changes and eliminate some things from my list, so I could leave room for Jesus.

BLESSED IS THE HEART
THAT MAKES ROOM FOR THE BABE

at Christmas.

Rewind with me to that very first Christmas. The shepherds were simply keeping watch over their flocks when the news arrived that Jesus was born. They were simply tending to their flocks, keeping their regular routine when great things occurred.

"And there were shepherds living out in the fields nearby, keeping watch over their flocks at night. An angel of the Lord appeared to them, and the glory of the Lord shone around them, and they were terrified.
But the angel said to them, "Do not be afraid. I bring you good news that will cause great joy for all the people. Today in the town of David a Savior has been born to you; he is the Messiah, the Lord. This will be a sign to you: You will find a baby wrapped in cloths and lying in a manger."
Luke 2:8-12 NIV

The shepherds were following their regular routine, "keeping watch over their flocks," when the news arrived that Jesus was born. Keeping their regular routine without cookies, presents, lights, or barnyard cookouts and parties. They waited. They watched. And the Good News of a babe born in Bethlehem came!

Let's slow down, pause, rewind and remember.

- Slow down and watch over your flock (just our daily routine)

- When the to do list is the size of Santa's list, pause and ask yourself what can be eliminated.

- Rewind and remember. Read Luke 2:1-20 with fresh eyes leaving room for the awareness of His presence.

MAKING ROOM

- In the wait, soften the noise of the world, and look for The King.

- Listen for the joy. The sound of His voice in His word as you open the Bible.

- Slow the haste. Rest in the comfort of His presence as you get alone to pray.

- Remember the goodness of a babe, born on Christmas Day, and praise His name.

- In the twinkle of the lights, remember the Light of the world.

- In the sweetness of the baked goods, remember the giver of all things good.

I'm certain the Birthday Boy will welcome jingle and increase joy as we make much over Him.

JOY TO THE WORLD THE *Lord* HAS COME

Lord HELP US *reach out* SO NO ONE WALKS ALONE THROUGH *grief*

amen

PRAY FOR THOSE WHO ARE GRIEVING

There's an angel I hang on my tree. It used to sit in my granny's bedroom. The first Christmas without her was hard; we said good-bye just weeks before Christmas.

Down the road there is a widow who will spend her first Christmas alone, a mom and dad who mourn the loss of a child not born, and parents who ache from losing their adult child just before Christmas.

Grief is hard. *"Jesus wept"* (John 11:35). He cried tears of loss, like you and me. He understands, and He wants us to bring our tears to Him.

He is Our comforter

*"All praise to God, the Father of our Lord Jesus Christ.
God is our merciful Father and the source of all comfort.
He comforts us in all our troubles so that we can comfort others."*
2 Corinthians 1:3-4 NLT

Grief was meant to be shared (Romans 12:15). We can share in the grief of another by listening when they share their heartaches or when they reminisce over a lost loved one. We can share their grief by remembering them after a loss. In the book of John, chapter 11, we find that Jesus goes to Mary and Martha to comfort them in their time of loss. Others were also present walking with these sisters in their grief.

Prayer can embrace a friend we can not physically reach in a time of grief.

Surround those who are aching this season with your love and prayers. Reach out, invite someone over, write a card. Let them know they are not alone.

How can we pray for those grieving?
- Ask God to be their comfort.
- Ask God to surround them with love and support.
- Ask God to be their strength when they feel weak.
- Ask God to show you how and when to reach out to the grieving.

Lord, You sent your son to walk this earth, to experience everything we do. He shed tears. He grieved. He cried with his friends over death, even with the promise of life eternally. You understand. Be the great comforter to those whose hearts ache from loss! Be strength and life to the hurting. Help us reach out so that no one walks alone through grief. Amen.

· · · · · *day 8*

Lord HELP STUDENTS *grow* IN WISDOM, STATURE & IN *favor* WITH GOD & MAN

amen

PRAY FOR STUDENTS

Young, old, and in between. Being a student comes with many challenges. Stress, desire to over perform, comparisons, financial burdens, time away from home and family. Odds are, we have all been a student, and perhaps we still are. Reflect on the challenges that come with learning, to help you pray.

Jesus himself was a student before he was a teacher. In Luke 2:46, *"...they found him in the temple courts, sitting among the teachers, listening to them and asking them questions."*

The story continues telling us that everyone was amazed because he had great understanding. Jesus was an attentive and inquisitive student who later become a wise teacher, one we still learn from today. Today we can also learn from his mother, Mary, who treasured her son and his time as a student (Luke 2:51) and understood that it was growing Jesus, *"in wisdom and stature, and in favor with God and man"* (Luke 2:52).

Luke 2:52 is a verse we can pray over students of all ages, those 12, like Jesus in the story mentioned, and those entering their first year of school and those taking off for college.

How can we pray for a student?
- Ask God to remove fears that interfere with going to school.
- Ask God to give them a good support system, family and friends that encourage.
- Ask God to give them the ability to understand instruction.
- Ask God to help them make wise choices when faced with peer pressure.
- Ask God to open doors to opportunities that help them learn and prepare for the future.

STUDENTS

Lord, thank you for giving us minds that can learn. We are born curious and become students almost immediately. Help students grow in wisdom, in stature and in favor of God and man. Help them deal with the stressors they face. Encourage their hearts. Keep them in your watch always, protecting them from peer pressure and physical harm. In Jesus' name, Amen.

day 9

Lord
LET OUR
hearts
BE
BURDENED
FOR *anyone*
WHO
DOES NOT
know YOU

amen

Jingle and Joy ~ Praying Beneath the Tree

PRAY FOR THE LOST TO KNOW JESUS

"For God so loved the world that He gave His only begotten Son,
that whoever believes in Him should not perish but have
everlasting life. For God did not send His Son into the world
to condemn the world, but that the world through
Him might be saved."
John 3:16-17 NIV

For those who know Jesus, December is a time of celebration while
others are left wondering and doubting. Perhaps they have heard
about Jesus, but don't believe. Perhaps they have not been told.
Pray that the Good News will reach their ears. Pray for the lost to
know and believe in Jesus.

I am reminded of an encounter I had at a gas pump when I began
writing this devotional. A gentleman approached me and asked if I
celebrated Christmas and wanted to share with me why I should
not. I listened a few moments, shared my faith in Jesus as best I
could, and left for my travels. But I didn't leave the same, I left with
a burden.

ASK GOD TO GIVE YOU A

burden for the lost this Christmas.

A burden that drives you to your knees in prayer for those who
haven't accepted Jesus as their Savior.

As you pray, also ask God to give you boldness for Him. A boldness
that drives you to love others by sharing the Good News with them.
Ask for a boldness that helps you embrace them with love

SALVATION

How can we pray for the lost?

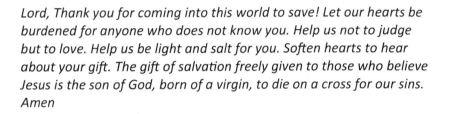

- Pray that the Good News will reach their ears.
- Pray for their hearts to be softened to receive the invitation of salvation through Jesus.
- Pray for them to experience the love of others this Christmas, so that they see Jesus.
- Pray they are not trapped in doubt and are set free accepting the love of Christ for themselves.

Lord, Thank you for coming into this world to save! Let our hearts be burdened for anyone who does not know you. Help us not to judge but to love. Help us be light and salt for you. Soften hearts to hear about your gift. The gift of salvation freely given to those who believe Jesus is the son of God, born of a virgin, to die on a cross for our sins. Amen

LORD

WE *Trust* YOU TO DO *great* THINGS

amen

PRAY FOR THE SICK

Almost every day we hear of someone in need of healing, from small colds to terminal diagnoses, the sick need our prayers.

1 Timothy 2:1, our focal verse, urges us to pray FIRST. Before we rush over with food, before we offer medicines and advice, we are urged to pray.

An online follower of the prayer tree posted her thoughts about prayer. She said, "Pray big," reminding us that Luke 1:37 says, ***"Nothing is impossible with God"***.

CANCER SEEMS BIG.

Our Creator is bigger.

Pray big prayers for the sick. It's ok to ask for healing. We often decide, without realizing, that the doctor's words are final, and we pray according to their prognosis. Even after the doctors give their word, God's word stands. He still performs miracles. He can do the impossible.

Pray big. Trust big.

> *"The earnest prayer of a righteous person has*
> *great power and produces wonderful results."*
> James 5:16b NLT

While you pray, remember your big may differ from another's big but our big God is bigger than any illness of this world.

Lord, Thank you for hearing our prayers. We lift those who are sick and in need of healing to you. Help us to remember to pray for them and with them. We trust you to do great things. Strengthen the sick. Give wisdom to their doctors. We know miracles are in your hands. We also know that beautiful, perfect healing is with you in heaven. No more suffering and no more pain. Thank you for that promise. Amen.

Jingle and Joy ~ Praying Beneath the Tree

day 11

Lord

PROTECT
OUR *teachers*
& ENCOURAGE
THEM
TO KEEP
Serving IN
THEIR JOBS

amen

PRAY FOR THE TEACHERS

One day, while out shopping, I met a teacher. She was putting a little white tree and blue ornaments in her cart. I was looking for ornaments for the prayer tree. We struck up a conversation and I learned she was a kindergarten teacher in my hometown. She was going to place the little white tree on her desk at school.

My curiosity got the better of me and I wondered why she would purchase a tree so late. School would dismiss in just a few days for Christmas vacation. So, I inquired, and wow, I learned things have really changed since I was an elementary student.

Her tree was white to celebrate "winter wonderland," rather than Christmas. She explained there was a long list of "do's and don'ts" for her to use in the classroom to avoid offending those who may not celebrate Christmas. Here I thought her biggest concern would be taming the excitement of overactive, sugar-filled little ones. I admired listening to her subtle ways of sharing God's love with the children. Her heart was warm, loving, and kind.

Teachers have the pressure of performing, they also have dozens of people to please. They have little ones in their care all day. They are disrespected and often ridiculed by their students and the parents of their students. And yes, they also must worry about how they share their beliefs in the classroom.

Teachers need our prayers. They also need our love, support, and encouragement. While you pray for teachers this week, would you also reach out to a teacher and encourage them? Write a kind note, drop off a small gift or baked goods. Let them know you see them and value their work. Give them your support.

"So encourage each other and build each other up"
1 Thessalonians 5:11 NLT

Lord, Jesus was a teacher. He too was ridiculed and disrespected. He continued to love others. He continued to teach. He loved children. He welcomed them with loving arms and tender words. Such a great example. We don't need lights and trees to share the good news. We need love, kind words, and open arms. The light that shines in us will draw others to you. Help our teachers be light in the darkness of legislation that constrains. Protect them and encourage them to keep loving and serving in the jobs you have placed them. Help us be an encouragement to a teacher this week. Amen

day 12

Lord

WE PRAY
FOR *provision*
& SAFETY
FOR
EACH PERSON
ON *Mission*

amen

PRAY FOR MISSIONARIES

They leave their homes, take time away from their jobs, travel away from their families, or uproot their families from all that is familiar. Some enter foreign countries. Others enter foreign neighborhoods to which no one would dare go. They make sacrifices, big and small. They are missionaries.

The Bible says, *"How beautiful on the mountains are the feet of the messenger who brings good news, the good news of peace and salvation, the news that the God of Israel reigns!"* (Isaiah 52:7 NLT). Next to this verse in my Bible I have written the name of a missionary family.

During December many churches and organizations collect items and money to help those who are living on mission full time. Today, and every day, we can offer them the gift of prayer.

Prayer is the gift that travels around the world free of cost. Prayer intercedes on the behalf of others. Prayer has the power to encourage the hearts of those who go and tell and softens the hearts of those who will hear the Good News. Prayer is the gift that changes things!

Pray for missionaries to:
- Be encouraged when they meet others who are different and don't respond positively.
- Have strength to persevere on days they feel depleted and drained.
- Have their basic needs of food, water, shelter, and healthcare met.
- Have protection from harm.
- Have time to refresh and refill.
- Be free of fear.

MISSIONARIES

Lord, How beautiful are the feet that tell the good news! They are faithful and courageous, loving and compassionate! They are also tired and worn. We pray for provision and safety for each person on mission. Provide for their basic needs, but also for the things they long to have to help share your love. Protect their homes from storms, their health from disease, and their minds from fear. Give us opportunities to be generous in our support. May we respond in faith. Amen

Each one of us has been called to tell about Jesus. We can be on mission in our own backyards. As you pray for those in full time mission work, also ask God to help you discover ways you can be on mission in your neighborhood.

day 13

Lord

BE REST
FOR *weary*
THE

& *strength*

FOR
THE WEAK

amen

PRAY FOR CARETAKERS

It takes special, selfless people to be caretakers.

They comfort the hurting, sit with the sick all through the night, sacrifice their time, and give themselves to others every day. Often their own lives are put on hold to attend to the needs of others.

They care BIG and ask for little in return.

My mom is a caretaker. Being present in a time of need is certainly her gift. She has been there for her children when they have given birth to her grandchildren. Not just to celebrate, but to do the things that need doing. Laundry, cooking, cleaning, burping, rocking, and yes, the dirty diapers. She has taken the night shift to sit bedside with the dying, opened her home to care for those with dementia and cancer. Observing her sacrifice has given me a greater understanding of a caretaker's need for prayer.

Caretakers are a special breed, you might say, often giving more than they ever receive. They need strength to press forward when days and nights grow long and weary. They need time to take care of personal needs while putting the needs of others first. They need help with income when they take time away from work.

How can we pray for caretakers?

- Pray that they are strengthened through rest and support from others.
- Pray for their health to remain good as they provide care.
- Pray for opportunities to present themselves for time away to care for their own needs.
- Pray for employers to be supportive of their need for time away.
- Pray for wisdom as their make decisions for others.

*"Come to me, all you who are weary and burdened,
and I will give you rest."*
Matthew 11:28 NIV

Lord, You are loving, kind and compassionate. Today we lift caregivers to you and ask that you wrap your love around them. It's a hard and strenuous job. May we each look for ways to help those who help others. Lord be rest to the weary and strength to the weak. In Jesus name, Amen.

day 14

Week Three

Exchange Presents for Presence

One year after Christmas my husband simply said, "Don't do that again."

I understood, and he was right. A large credit card bill arrived in the mail and I admit, I was disappointed in myself. Somewhere in the jingle of Christmas I purchased too much and now I would pay the price, literally.

Have you been there? Your intentions are good. You want to share your love for others during the Christmas season by giving gifts but instead of sharing joy with others, you excite the retailers and overextend your bank account.

THIS YEAR EXCHANGE PRESENTS FOR PRESENCE.

Give less from the store and more from your heart. Take the time that you would spend shopping and spend it with loved ones and even strangers by taking time to volunteer. Instead of spending money for gifts, spend time in prayer asking how you can offer your presence to Him and others during this season.

Many gifts can be given freely, without tissue paper, bags and bows. These gifts far outweigh presents that require wrapping!

Here are four gifts to consider that don't require tape, tissue, or tags:

♦ COMFORT

Grief seems to multiply during the holiday season.

2 Corinthians 1:3-4 proclaims that our Father God is the God of all comfort and those who have received His comfort are able to comfort others.

The best way I know to be of comfort to someone is to first pray for them and then be present.

Sit quietly when they need you near. Send cards, make phone calls, and just let them know they are not alone. Cry when they cry and laugh when they laugh. Your presence will speak to their heart in ways that presents often fall short.

♦ TIME

Yikes, right! Time? It ticks away faster than we can blink. Everyone agrees. How on earth can we suggest a gift of time? Especially when we all have Decemberitis! Yes, Decemberitis. It's a disease that begins the day after Thanksgiving and lasts until about January 2nd. It seems to affect most of us.

Jesus took time in his final days to spend with his closest friends.

"Jesus knew that his hour had come to leave this world and return to his Father. He had loved his disciples during his ministry on earth, and now he loved them to the very end. It was time for supper..."
John 13:1-2 NLT

In His final days, the time drawing near to His death, Jesus chose to spend time with friends. Sharing a meal. Sharing love. Sharing important time and valuable teachings. He took time. He gave time.

We can't slow the clock, but we can choose how to spend our time. Rather than racing through stores and scanning sales online we can offer presence over presents.

With less time spent looking for the perfect gift to buy, we will have more time to offer others. This year consider how you spend your time and look for ways to be present.

Run errands for a single mom or elderly widow. Offer to cook, wrap gifts, or clean for someone who is sick. Volunteer at a shelter or other service aiding others during Christmas. Simply slow down and linger longer at the dinner table with your family. Dine together. Laugh together. Cry together.

TIME CANNOT BE BOUGHT

but it is priceless

WHEN WELL SPENT TOGETHER.

◆ PRAYER

Of course, I must mention praying for others. Prayer is an invaluable gift. Its priceless value far exceeds our wildest imagination! Blessings abound when we drop to our knees and lift our voices up to Jesus. God has the ability and the desire to hear each request and to attend to every need (review Day 1).

One special way you can pray for others this season is praying scripture. Almost any need we can imagine has a scripture that relates.

Does your friend need strength? Pray for God's power to be their strength.

But he said to me, "My grace is sufficient for you, for my power is made perfect in weakness." Therefore I will boast all the more gladly about my weaknesses, so that Christ's power may rest on me.
2 Corinthians 12:9 NIV

Does your friend need peace? Pray for God's peace to consume their heart.

"And the peace of God, which surpasses all understanding, will guard your hearts and your minds in Christ Jesus." Philippians 4:7 NIV

Consider a friend's need and carry it to the Lord. It's the gift we cannot place a value upon.

This year, as the tug of war between the world and our heart ensues, choose presence over presents.

QUIET THE *jingle* & USHER IN THE *joy*

Lord
CONSUME
OUR *Hearts*
WITH
PEACE

amen

PRAY FOR PEACE (INNER)

We are 15 days into our journey beneath the tree. Praying over "all" can seem overwhelming. Hopefully breaking it into defined categories is paving a way to navigate praying for others without creating unnecessary worry or anxiety.

When I wrote the words "pray for peace" I paused to wonder what others would perceive of this prompt. Would they consider nations ceasing to wage war against one another? Perhaps. Would they pray for relationships to be healed and restored? Perhaps.

Then I remembered the truth we find in God's word in 2 Corinthians 4:8-9 NIV,

"We are hard pressed on every side, but not crushed; perplexed, but not in despair; persecuted, but not abandoned; struck down, but not destroyed."

And Jesus' words in John 16:33 NIV,

"...In this world you will have trouble."

So, knowing this, how can I expect, with the troubles that mount against us and haunt us, that we would achieve peace?

BECAUSE JESUS TRUMPS THE TROUBLES OF THIS WORLD!

He is greater.

He is also the giver of peace. Just as He can calm waves with a word, he can also calm our hearts and minds while the waves still crash around us.

"I am leaving you with a gift—peace of mind and heart.
And the peace I give is a gift the world cannot give.
So don't be troubled or afraid."
John 14: 27 NLT

Today we pray for inner peace; peace within our minds and hearts. Peace even when things press in on us. Peace that consumes and rules our hearts (Colossians 3:15).

Lord, You are the giver of great things. Love and joy are found in your presence. You are also the giver of peace. Help us grasp the gift of peace you offer. We know that there will be trouble; help us trust that you are greater than all the troubles of this world. Consume our hearts with peace. Amen .

day 15

Lord
HOLD
FIRST RESPONDER'S
families
UNDER THE
SAFETY
OF
YOUR *wings*

amen

PRAY FOR THOSE
SERVING IN THE MILITARY

There is no greater gift you can give those serving in the military than to be in constant prayer for them and their families.

While my husband was overseas for a year, prayer held us together. Prayer was our lifeline. Prayer was able to bridge the gap that distance created. Prayer gave us hope. Prayer brought us peace. No matter how many boxes I shipped filled with food and thoughts of home, prayer was the most priceless gift I could offer my husband.

I ONCE READ THAT WHEN WE PRAY

we build bridges

BETWEEN GOD AND HIS PEOPLE.

Being a wife of a soldier, I can attest to this as truth. Prayer traveled the distance I could not. I always trusted God to be with my husband and in all situations at home. Claiming the words of Psalm 18:29 helped me rest in the peace that only God can provide.

> *"In your strength I can crush an army;*
> *with my God I can scale any wall."* Psalm 18:29

God's word reminded me that my husband was not alone.

Many servicemen and women will spend Christmas away from those they love. We can pray that they always feel the presence of God with them. The Father gives us an open door to intercede on behalf of others. Let us be their prayer warriors while they are our warriors helping to provide the freedom we enjoy.

MILITARY

How can we pray for our military?

- Pray for their wellbeing. This includes physical, mental, and spiritual health.
- Pray for their families to have support when they are absent.
- Pray for their marriages to remain strong.
- Pray for their children who grieve their absence.
- Pray for their leadership to make wise choices.

Lord, You are faithful! We praise you. We fall short and there is turmoil, disagreement, and evil around us. There are those who say, "I will serve to protect." We lift them to you. Be their constant protection. Bring swiftness to their feet. Keep their minds alert and sharp. Hold their families under the safety of your wings. Amen

day 16

Lord FILL THE *lonely* WITH THE JOY THAT ONLY COMES FROM *above*

amen

Jingle and Joy ~ Praying Beneath the Tree

PRAY FOR THE LONELY

The holiday season is especially hard for those who are overwhelmed with loneliness. I recall the first time I read Psalm 68:6 NLT. I was praying for orphans. My eyes opened wide and my heart rejoiced as I read, ***"God places the lonely in families; he sets the prisoners free and gives them joy."***

God places the lonely in families.

I think we see this in many ways. God calls us His children. We have a father in Him. When His children extend their arms and embrace others, we too bring the lonely into families. Family.

Just last year we were able to open our home to a friend going through a difficult divorce. Both her children and all her family were many states away. No transportation was available and being together was impossible. She was overjoyed to celebrate with us and we were overjoyed to have her. Family.

When my husband and I moved to a new town as a newly married couple we searched for a church home. The search led us to a small group consisting of young couples all living in a town away from their families. We bonded, helping one another in times of need, celebrating special occasions, studying the word together each week. Family.

This Christmas, pray for the lonely. Pray they know Jesus loves them. Look for ways to share time with others and even to invite someone alone to be part of your family celebrations. Visit a nursing home and spend time with someone who has no visitors. Visit a shut in. Serve in a shelter, if you can.

Most of all remember our verse, **"I urge you first of all, to pray for all people."** 1 Timothy 2:1 NLT.

Lord, You are a good Father. Thank you for calling us your children. We are not alone. But we long for others to share relationships with and it's difficult when we feel alone and abandoned. Place the lonely in families. Fill them with joy that comes from above. Amen .

day 17

Lord
WE
LIFT THOSE
IN *high*
places
TO
YOU

amen

Jingle and Joy ~ Praying Beneath the Tree

PRAY FOR OUR LEADERS

Remember our focal scripture, 1 Timothy 2:1? We have talked at length about praying first for all people. We have mentioned many groups, and most are not what I would consider controversial.

Now let's read 1 Timothy 2:1-3 NLT:
"I urge you, first of all, to pray for all people. Ask God to help them; intercede on their behalf, and give thanks for them. Pray this way for kings and all who are in authority so that we can live peaceful and quiet lives marked by godliness and dignity. This is good and pleases God our Savior."

Praying for ALL people includes ALL who are in authority. Those who are in authority are the leaders we find in our community, our state, and our country. They are also in our churches and workplaces. We are instructed to pray for all of them, regardless of our opinions. I know. It may feel like I am meddling instead of encouraging at this point. But hang with me.

Consider the result of our prayers.

Verse three states we intercede on their behalf "So that we can live peaceful and quiet lives marked by godliness and dignity." I do not want to get "political", but perhaps, just perhaps, it's less about us agreeing with what those in authority do, and don't do, and more about how we pray for them.

- Pray for those in authority in your community.
- Pray for those in authority in our country.
- Pray for those in authority in our churches.
- Pray for all those in authority.

LEADERS

Lord, We lift those in high places to you...the Highest Authority. We simply ask you to help them. Help them to remember you and your ways as they lead. Let us support them faithfully through intercessory prayer. Amen.

day 18

Lord

LET US

encourage

SOMEONE &

MAKE A

DIFFERENCE

IN THEIR

day

amen

PRAY FOR RETAIL WORKERS

Six days before Christmas, and many will race and rush to purchase gifts. Stress will build as lines get long, coupons fail to work, sizes run out, and people forget their manners.

Things will be said and done toward those who are doing their very best to provide a service. Tempers will rise, and words will be spewed in their direction for problems they haven't caused and that they are unable to fix. I know, because I have not only witnessed this but, unfortunately, I have been the disgruntled shopper taking my stress out on an overworked cashier.

Retail workers will work long hours, sacrifice time with their families, and endure undue pressure to perform "miracles."

Let's pray for them today.

And while you are out and about, smile a little extra, say thank you as much as you can, let someone go in front of you, if they seem in a hurry. Do what you can to help others keep tensions down and spirits up. Carry this verse with you along the way,

"My dear brothers and sisters, take note of this: Everyone should be quick to listen, slow to speak and slow to become angry."
James 1:19 NIV

Lord, We get so busy in this season. So busy that we forget what we are celebrating. We forget your instructions to be kind, compassionate, and loving toward others. Forgive us. Today we pray for those in retail during the busiest shopping season. Give them strength, keep their health well, and encourage their hearts when others act out toward them. Let us also be an encouragement and make a difference in their day! Amen.

RETAIL WORKERS

LET'S
PRAY
today

Jingle and Joy ~ Praying Beneath the Tree

day 19

LORD *Help us*
IN OUR WEAKNESSES,
BE THE *Strength*
WE NEED TO
overcome

amen

Jingle and Joy ~ Praying Beneath the Tree

PRAY FOR THOSE WHO BATTLE ADDICTIONS

Each day lives are destroyed as addictions take hold and win. Marriages suffer, jobs are lost, bodies are plagued with crippling health effects, and many lose their lives. Young and old, rich and poor, all are affected. My own family is not immune and likely yours isn't either.

We often limit our thoughts on addiction to someone dependent on drugs and alcohol, forgetting that there are many substances, things, and activities that can be habit-forming and detrimental. While drugs and alcohol are common, many suffer from addictions to food, pornography, gambling, sex, shopping, video games, internet use, and the list goes on.

Odds are if you just read that list you are thinking of someone, perhaps even yourself, that struggles with addiction. This is a battle and we have a weapon. Prayer. We can intercede in prayer and we can reach out to offer help and to receive help. Offering help is not overstepping, requesting help is not a sign of weakness.

"Dear brothers and sisters, if another believer is overcome by some sin, you who are godly should gently and humbly help that person back onto the right path. And be careful not to fall into the same temptation yourself. Share each other's burdens, and in this way obey the law of Christ."
Galatians 6:1-2 NLT

O Lord, I have come to you for protection; don't let me be disgraced. Save me, for you do what is right. Turn your ear to listen to me; rescue me quickly. Be my rock of protection, a fortress where I will be safe."
Psalm 31:1-2 NLT

How can we pray for those battling addiction?

- Ask God to give them courage to reach out for help.
- Ask God to protect their health during the battle.
- Ask God to deliver them from their stronghold.
- Ask God to restore them as only He can.
- Ask God to place others in their lives that can stand beside them in the battle.

Lord, Our flesh fails, and we give in to things that grab hold of us and won't let go. Help us in our weaknesses. Be the strength we need to overcome the things that wage war against our minds and bodies. Be strength to the one who wants so desperately to overcome addiction. Let us race to their side and support them in prayer, love, and encouragement. Amen.

day 20

Week Four

Let Christmas Linger

Just a few days after Christmas one year I read a post on Facebook, "Christmas, it's all put away."

My friend was excited, and my heart sank. I understood the post, I did. I knew what she meant; she had a feeling of accomplishment. The tree was down, the clutter of gatherings was cleared. Christmas was "put away."

Now, I'm not here to ask you to leave out your decorations, but join me in letting Christmas linger.

Linger in adoration of the One whose birth we celebrate.
Linger in the bravery of a virgin Mary.
Linger in the faith of Joseph.
Linger in the miracle of a virgin birth.
Linger in the Hope of Jesus!

We rush to and through Christmas many times. Hopefully, this year was different for you. Put away the urge to begin rushing now that the world is pushing toward New Year's resolutions.

Mary, Jesus' mother, and the shepherds set the example for our hearts to follow as the New Year approaches.

"They hurried to the village and found Mary and Joseph. And there was the baby, lying in the manger. After seeing him, the shepherds told everyone what had happened and what the angel had said to them about this child. All who heard the shepherds' story were astonished, but Mary kept all these

things in her heart and thought about them often.
The shepherds went back to their flocks, glorifying and
praising God for all they had heard and seen. It was just
as the angel had told them."
Luke 2:16-20 NLT

The shepherds came in a hurry! They celebrated by telling everyone the good news! Then they returned to their work, praising God. We have come, we have seen, now we can return to our work, telling others the good news, and praising Jesus throughout the New Year.

And Mary. Sweet Mary, she kept all these things in her heart!

And thought of them often!

May we, like the shepherds, return to our flocks, with a heart like Mary!

A heart filled with Jesus.

Think of Him often,
tell others of His goodness,
praise Him every day.

LET CHRISTMAS LINGER.

LET CHRISTMAS LINGER

Lord
COME
quickly
TO THOSE
WHO ARE
in a pit
OF
DEPRESSION

amen

Jingle and Joy ~ Praying Beneath the Tree

PRAY FOR THOSE STRUGGLING
WITH DEPRESSION

She picked up the phone and I could hear in her voice, she was crying. I inquired asking, "What was the matter?" to which she responded, "I don't know." My heart understood. Sometimes nothing is wrong. Other times it seems everything is wrong. Either way, depression rears its ugly head and consumes many.

My friend would later be okay, but not until depression was diagnosed, treated, and the battle was fought. Many years later when another friend was hospitalized with the same diagnosis I knew exactly what to do. I turned to God's word in prayer. I opened my bible and wrote my friends name next to Psalm 143:7-8 and the words became my heart's cry for her life.

Psalm 143:7-8 NIV reads,
"Answer me quickly, Lord; my spirit fails.
Do not hide your face from me or
I will be like those who go down to the pit.
Let the morning bring me word of your unfailing love,
for I have put my trust in you.
Show me the way I should go, for to you I entrust my life."

I inserted her name in several places throughout these verses. Many mornings I would simply whisper, *"Lord, Lift Connie from the pit and let her feel your unfailing love."* This became a powerful way to pray for her and later, others.

Depression hurts. It leaves deep scars.

IT IS LIKE A DARK CLOUD THAT OFTEN
COMES WITHOUT WARNING.

DEPRESSION

How can we pray for those suffering from depression?

- Pray that they talk to someone and find medical care, if needed.
- Pray that others surround them with love and support.
- Pray that they feel God's love each morning.
- Pray they have strength as they battle this disease.

Lord, Hear our cry. Come quickly to those who are down in a pit we call depression. Let them hear your loving voice each morning. Be their anchor of hope as they trust in you. Protect their life and fill their hearts with joy. In Jesus' name, Amen.

day 21

Lord

HELP US

TO *work* WITH A

joyful

SPIRIT
IN ALL THAT
WE DO

amen

PRAY FOR A CO-WORKER

We work together, spending almost as much time together, if not more, than we do with family. Work environments can be filled with tension and stress daily. We can often get caught in behaviors such as gossip, complaining, and competition that create office friction and harm one another.

PRAYER CAN BE THE CATALYST FOR

positive change in the workplace.

This week as you venture out to work, consider praying for your co-workers by name before you leave home. As you pray, ask for everyone to have respect for one another. Remember your bosses, asking God to give them wisdom and good leadership skills (refer to Day 18). At work, pray during the day as you walk by each person's office or chair.

Pray for yourself as well. Pray that you would be kind, considerate, and share the workload with joy. Ask God to help you be an encouragement to others. Remember that God's instruction for being gentle, patient, and loving (Ephesians 4:2) is as applicable at work as they are at home or church.

While you may not always be able to pray with one another, if the opportunity presents have courage to pray together.

Consider the words of Colossians 3:23 NIV as you enter the workplace with a prayerful attitude.

> *"Whatever you do, work at it with all your heart,*
> *as working for the Lord, not for human masters."*

CO-WORKER

Lord, Help us to work with a joyful spirit in all that we do. Help us shine your light in our workplaces, remembering to pray for one another. We rejoice now for replacing stress and tension with love and kindness. Thank you for being with us wherever we go, including work. When our co-workers notice a change, let us rejoice in you. Amen.

day 22

Lord
WE
need you
IN THIS
SIN-
SOAKED
world

amen

PRAY FOR THE FRAGILE

The elderly.
The sick.
The broken.
The hurting.
The marriage struggling.
The addict crumbling.
The prodigal wandering.
The lost that are wavering.
Those fragile things that need tender prayer.

Spend time reflecting on the tender moment of Jesus being born.

> *"She gave birth to her firstborn, a son.*
> *She wrapped him in cloths and placed him in a manger,*
> *because there was no room for them."*
> Luke 2:7 NIV

Imagine Mary, young, away from home, her first child being birthed among animals. She herself may have felt fragile, afraid, or alone. Joseph could encourage her, but even he could not fully understand all her needs. This was fragile.

I'm reminded of boxes coming and going through the mail at Christmas. Large red lettering reads "Handle with Care,"a note for everyone handling the package to be gentle. Could we see the words this way, "Handle with Prayer"?

Think about those you may know who are struggling and be tender and gentle, lifting them to our compassionate Father. Handle each one with prayer.

FRAGILE

Lord, In every corner of the world there is a need. We need you in this fragile, sin-soaked world. You made a way! Praise! The fragile infant Mary wrapped in cloths came to endure suffering for us. Open our eyes and hearts to receive Jesus. To make room for Him. We welcome Him into our fragile lives. The hard parts of our own life. And yes, we pray for all to receive Him! Where there is Jesus, the weak become strong! Be with every man, woman, and child. Meet them in their fragile. Strengthen them from within. Glory to God in the highest! Amen .

Lord

HELP US
TO OFFER

forgiveness

TO THOSE
WHO HAVE
HURT US

amen

PRAY FOR FORGIVENESS

One of my favorite Christmas movies, *Home Alone*, contains an older male character that lives alone in the house next door to the main character's bustling home filled with children and Christmas cheer. As the story unfolds, it becomes clear that the young boy living next door is afraid of this older fella. As the movie progresses we learn the older neighbor is also home alone at Christmas because of a disagreement with his son. We do get a happy ending in this film as the older man is reunited with his son and it is clear a wrong or misunderstanding has been forgiven.

Do you find it hard to understand how families and friendships become so broken? Or do you understand completely because you live with the pain of a broken relationship in need of forgiveness? Christmas is the perfect season for us to consider forgiveness; after all, the birth of Jesus that we celebrate occurred so that the death of Jesus could cover all our sins.

Jesus was born to die. His death was to provide life, eternal life. The gift of eternity with Jesus comes when we trust that He is God's only Son who came to die for our sins.

"For God so loved the world that he gave his one and only Son,
that whoever believes in him shall not perish but have eternal life.
For God did not send his Son into the world to condemn the world,
but to save the world through him."
John 3:16-17 NIV

In the book of Romans, we read that we are all sinners in need of forgiveness (Romans 3:23) and that the wages of sin is death. But we have a God of forgiveness. One that does not want a broken relationship with us, He offers forgiveness and restoration (Acts 3:19).

God forgives, & he asks us to do the same.

*"Make allowance for each other's faults, and forgive
anyone who offends you. Remember, the Lord forgave you,
so you must forgive others."*
Colossians 3:13 NLT

Today ask yourself honestly, "Is there anything I need to confess before the Lord, asking for forgiveness? Is there anyone I need to forgive personally?" As you answer these questions pray knowing that
God provided a way for all our sins to be forgiven and He also desires
us to forgive one another.

*Lord, We come falling before you as sinners, trusting that Jesus made
a way for our sins to be forgiven. Thank you. Forgive us of our sins.
Help us to offer forgiveness to those who have hurt us. Help us trust
that with you relationships that are broken can be healed and restored. In Jesus' name, Amen.*

· · · · · · day 24

Thank you
LORD
FOR
Sending
YOUR
Son

amen

Jingle and Joy ~ Praying Beneath the Tree

PRAISE GOD FOR CHRISTMAS

"While they were there, the time came for the baby to be born,
and she gave birth to her firstborn, a son.
She wrapped him in cloths and placed him in a manger,
because there was no guest room available for them."
Luke 2:6-7 NIV

"Today in the town of David a Savior has been born to you; he is
the Messiah, the Lord. This will be a sign to you: You will find a
baby wrapped in cloths and lying in a manger." Suddenly a great
company of the heavenly host appeared with the angel, praising
God and saying, "Glory to God in the highest heaven, and on earth
peace to those on whom his favor rests. When the angels had left
them and gone into heaven, the shepherds said to one another,
"Let's go to Bethlehem and see this thing that has happened,
which the Lord has told us about."
Luke 2: 11-15 NIV

"The shepherds returned, glorifying and praising
God for all the things they had heard and seen,
which were just as they had been told."
Luke 2:20 NIV

We've talked about the shepherds before. While doing their regular daily activities they were told about this child that would be born. They went to see what had happened. Then they returned, "glorifying and praising" God.

AS YOU PAUSE AND REFLECT
ON THAT FIRST CHRISTMAS,

praise God for sending His Son.

AS YOU PONDER THESE THINGS IN YOUR HEART, LIKE MARY,

praise God for His love.

AS YOU RETURN TO YOUR DAILY ACTIVITIES,

praise God for sending

A SPECIAL GIFT THAT VERY FIRST CHRISTMAS

The miracle of Christmas is a babe born of a virgin birth. He was born with a clear purpose. He was born to carry the weight of our sins to the cross. He was born to die on that cross for you and me, for all. He was born to give us a gift. That gift is called eternal life. It is a gift freely offered, but it must be accepted personally by each person.

Today praise God for Christmas. Not the season, but the birth of Jesus, the one and only son of God, born to save all.

Thank you, Lord, for sending your Son. Thank you for sending him to save ALL. He loves us all. He loves us just as we are. He came with a purpose. Thank you! We rejoice! We sing praise! Together we say hallelujah! Together we praise you for Jesus. Amen.

day 25

Lord
MAY OUR
prayers
BE
FILLED
WITH
compassion
AS WE WAIT
EXPECTANTLY
FOR YOUR
response

amen

Jingle and Joy ~ Praying Beneath the Tree

day 26 – 31

AFTER THE TREES ARE DOWN, CONTINUE PRAYING

Soon we will begin to pack away Christmas decorations. Trees will come down, ornaments will be placed gently in boxes, and pine needles will be vacuumed away. Our prayers can and should continue. We are urged to *"pray without ceasing"* in 1 Thessalonians 5:17. Put this verse into action as you remove your trees and commit to pray faithfully for others throughout next year.

Prayer ideas for the whole year:

- ◆ Keep your Christmas cards in a bowl and pray for someone each night as you take a card out and remember the sender.
- ◆ String a line for hanging prayer tags. Each day jot who or what you are praying for on a tag and clip it to the string. The reverse side can be used for praise when that prayer is answered!
- ◆ Keep a prayer journal. Write your prayers in one color, leaving space to come back and write your praises for answered prayers in another color.
- ◆ Use a calendar with daily prayer prompts.
- ◆ Find a prayer partner. Pick a day of the week to check in with one another and pray together.

Long after the last ornament is tucked away we want to continue to be faithful to pray. Rejoice in knowing the Lord does not take a single day off from hearing and responding to our prayers. His word proclaims, *"the earnest prayer of a righteous man produces wonderful results"* (James 5:16 NLT).

Continue to pray expectantly

TAKING YOUR REQUESTS TO HIM EACH MORNING.

AFTER CHRISTMAS

"In the morning, Lord, you hear my voice;
in the morning I lay my requests before you
and wait expectantly."
Psalm 5:3 NIV

Lord, You are good, and your love endures forever! We rejoice in knowing there is no time limit on how long we can pray. Help us be faithful to pray without ceasing for all people. We need you. Our world needs you. May our greatest desire be to live a life that expresses our love for you and our love for others. May our prayers be filled with compassion as we wait expectantly for your response. Amen.

day 26

day 27 · · · · · ·

day 29 · · · · · ·

day 31 · · · · · ·

Jodie Barrett is a girl who loves Jesus and sharing his word. Wife to Thomas, her high school sweetheart, mother to their children Ryan and Lauren, and ministry leader with Faithfully Following Ministries. Her passion is teaching women the Word of God, helping women unearth the treasure of God's love letter, verse by verse. She looks for joy in everyday things like laundry, waiting in line and cooking, considering each an opportunity to share God's love with others!

Catch up with Jodie and her ministry partner Donna Fender on their blog at FaithfullyFollowingMinistries.org.

Also from Jodie

Our world needs more joy!
Will you join us on a mission to deliver joy,
One Jar At A Time?

For more information visit
FaithfullyFollowingMinistries.org/one-jar-time/

True thanksgiving is so much more than a holiday or a by-product of changing seasons.

True thanksgiving is a heart condition displayed in our normal day to day life.

True thanksgiving is
everyday thanksgiving.

For more information visit
SweetToTheSoul.com/everydaythanksgiving.htm

Jingle and Joy ~ Praying Beneath the Tree

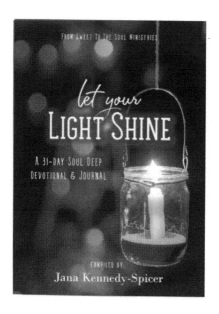

We live in a dark world, and it seems to be getting darker day by day. Fear, depression, grief, abuse, illness can seem overwhelming. But there is a hope. *There is a light.*

"Prayer and Bible study can flip a switch on in a dark room."
~ Jodie Barrett

For more information visit
SweetToTheSoul.com/let-your-light-shine.htm

Made in the USA
Middletown, DE
28 November 2018